❁ BIG ❁
EMBROIDERY

20 crewel embroidery designs to stitch with wool

NANCY NICHOLSON

sewandso

www.sewandso.co.uk

CONTENTS

INTRODUCTION

This is a book of ideas for using knitting and tapestry wool (yarn) for embroidery instead of the finer threads that you'd normally associate with this type of needlework. The skills and stitches required are much the same as with traditional embroidery, so if you're already an experienced embroiderer, you won't be starting from scratch. But chunkier threads mean you will be working on a larger scale, and you'll find that these projects are a great way to introduce beginners, including children, to the pleasures of hand-stitched embroidery.

Indeed, behind all the projects is the desire to share the joy of taking something familiar and giving it a new twist. For many of the projects I've used wool embroidery to embellish, customise and transform everyday garments – knitwear, jeans, slippers – as well as blankets, too. But there are ideas for making your own projects also, from belts to bags, cards to cushions, and purses to pictures. I have used leftover knitting and crochet yarns for many of the projects and the results are just as detailed and intricate as using traditional embroidery threads.

Above all, I want you to use these projects as a source of inspiration rather than as a rule book. While I have provided Embroidery Suggestions throughout for the designs as I have stitched them, I urge you to experiment, to combine stitches and motifs to create your own unique results. Just relax and enjoy your growing confidence. Remember, you can always unpick and start a small area again – I do this all the time!

With a comprehensive Stitch Library to refer to and motif spreads to inspire you, I hope you will apply your ideas to different textiles around your home, to any fabric where the weave is loose enough to accommodate the larger threads. Here's an invitation to play, to explore these pages and take the ideas into new places, just as I've done. It's an invitation to have some fun, so think big!

TOOLS AND MATERIALS

WOOL (YARN) AND OTHER THREADS

Knitting wool: I have most often used double knitting wool and sometimes a slightly finer 4-ply (fingering) wool, usually leftovers from knitting or crochet projects.

Tapestry wool: I use Anchor or Appletons yarn in either 2-ply or 4-ply. Tapestry wools are sold in skeins in many beautiful colours, but always start from your stash of leftovers. (You can often find unwanted embroidery kits or other remnants for very little money in charity shops.)

Laceweight wool: Whenever you want to embroider something more delicate this finer yarn is a good choice. I've used it for the embroidery on the mittens and the sash belt.

Fine crewel wool: Often provided in traditional shop-bought embroidery kits, this type of yarn is very similar to laceweight wool in the effect it gives.

Other threads: Don't be limited by the suggestions above. Once you have gained confidence by completing some of the projects here, allow yourself some freedom to experiment with ribbon, fabric strips and even string.

FABRICS

You can embroider on just about anything, so take a look at what you have to hand and experiment. Basically, if a needle will go through it, you can embroider it.

For the embroideries onto felt, I have used a 'heathered' felt that has a marled effect, so the colours are much more subtle than with nylon felts (see Suppliers). For the embroideries onto fabric, I've mostly used a heavyweight woollen or linen fabric.

Listed below are some suitable fabrics for big embroidery. They need to be a heavier weight than for ordinary embroidery and will usually be found in the upholstery section of fabric shops.

- Heavyweight woollen fabric
- Tweeds
- Heavyweight linen fabric (upholstery weight with an open weave)
- Boiled wool
- Thick felt
- Knitwear

NEEDLES

While it is always good to have a variety of needles in your sewing box, the types of needle you are most likely to use when working with wool (yarn) are tapestry and chenille. Clearly, your needle will need an eye large enough for the wool (yarn) you are using. I've used chenille size 21 mostly, but try a tapestry needle if you prefer a blunter end. Experiment until you find the one you like.

SCISSORS

You'll need a collection of good-quality scissors: a pair of general purpose scissors for cutting paper templates; a pair of dedicated fabric cutting scissors; and sharp embroidery scissors for snipping threads.

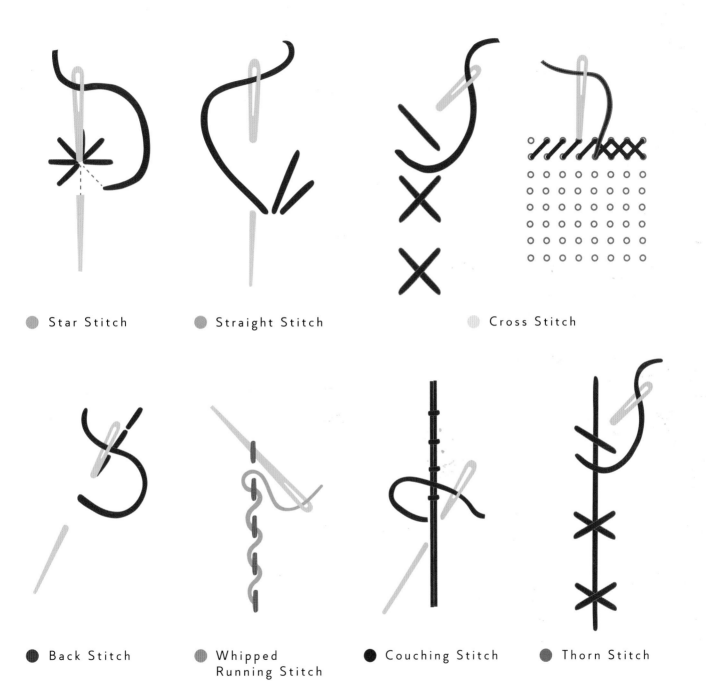

● Star Stitch

● Straight Stitch

● Cross Stitch

● Back Stitch

● Whipped Running Stitch

● Couching Stitch

● Thorn Stitch

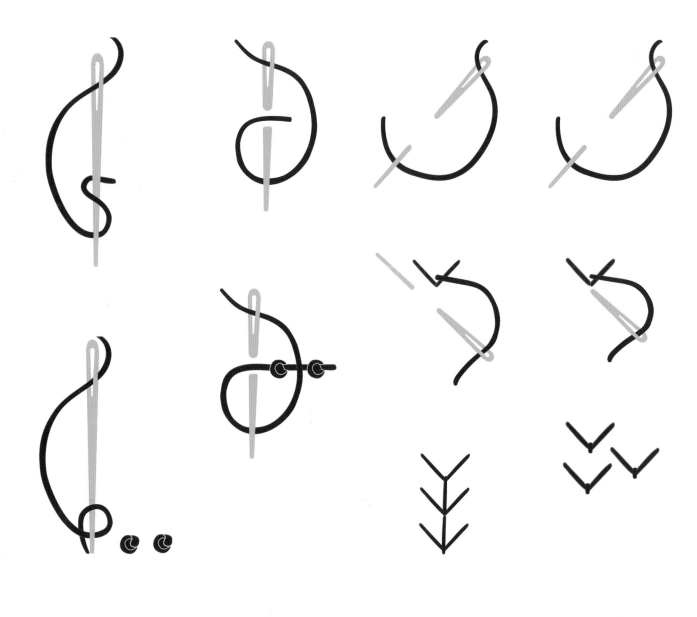

● French Knot　　　● Coral Stitch　　　● Fly Stitch　　　● Detached Fly Stitch

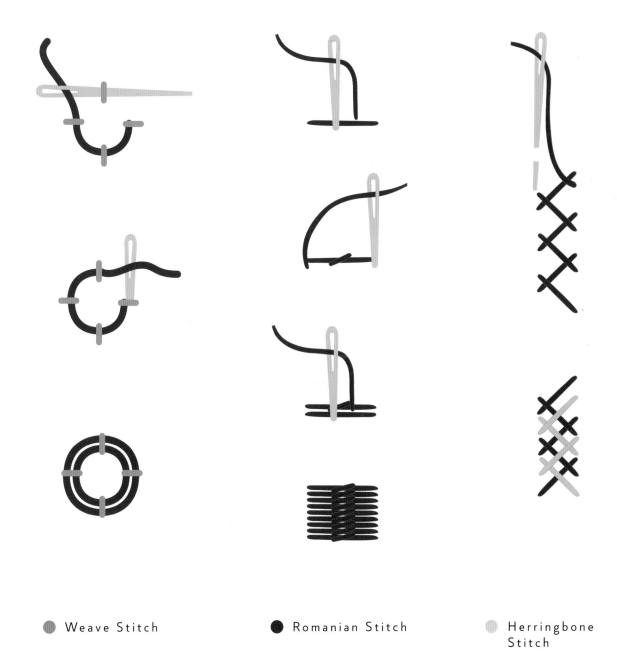

● Weave Stitch   ● Romanian Stitch   ● Herringbone Stitch

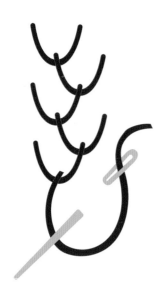

● Feather Stitch

● Stem Stitch

● Buttonhole Stitch

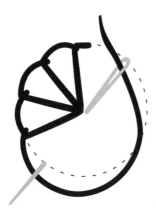

● Buttonhole
Wheel Stitch

● Buttonhole
Flower Stitch

● Satin Stitch

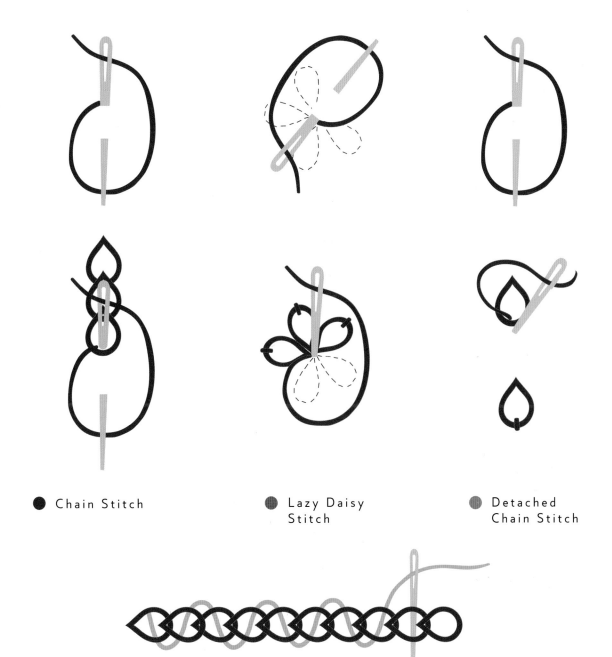

● Chain Stitch

● Lazy Daisy Stitch

● Detached Chain Stitch

● Laced Chain Stitch

PROJECTS

GREETING CARDS

There is nothing better than to receive a handmade greeting card, so why not make a few in readiness to send? These quick-to-stitch designs are a great way to practise lots of different embroidery stitches using all those yarn leftovers you have stashed away. And I hope they will inspire you to create your own radial patterns and flower motifs.

YOU WILL NEED

Double-fold cards with circle aperture measuring 7.5cm (3in)

10cm (4in) felt squares in a choice of colours

Oddments of knitting or tapestry wool (yarn) in a choice of colours

Adhesive tape (masking or washi)

Glue stick

MAKING UP

1. Take your double-fold card and open it out flat onto a piece of paper. Use a pencil to draw around the circle aperture onto the paper, then set aside the card. Cut out the marked circle from the paper and mark the stitching guidelines (see Techniques: Marking out a circular shape).

2. Take your felt square and fold it in half and half again to mark the centre point. Place a pin through the centre point of your paper circle and through the centre of the felt square, lining up the fold lines on the felt with the guidelines on the paper circle. Use a heat-erasable pen to mark the section guidelines around the edge of the circle, then remove the paper circle and use a ruler to join up the marked points to complete the transfer of the stitching guidelines to the felt.

3. Using tapestry or knitting wool (yarn), embroider your chosen design (see Embroidery Suggestions).

4. Once complete, use a damp cloth to press the finished embroidery to remove the stitching guidelines.

5. Take the set aside double-fold card and lay it front side down on your work surface. Place the embroidered felt square right side down over the circle aperture in the centre panel (it may be necessary to trim the edges of the felt square to fit). Making sure that the embroidery is centred in the aperture, fix it in place with adhesive tape. Fold the left-hand panel of the card over the back of the felt and glue in place to hide the back of the embroidery.

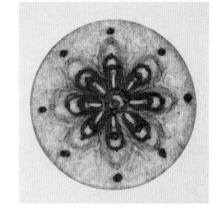
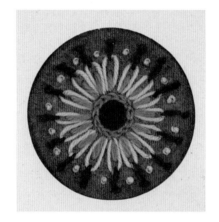

EMBROIDERY SUGGESTIONS

Embroider your design using the stitch suggestions displayed here. Refer to the Stitch Library for instructions for working the embroidery stitches.

- ● Detached Fly Stitch
- ● Detached Chain Stitch
- ● Satin Stitch
- ● French Knot
- ● Straight Stitch
- ● Weave Stitch
- ● Romanian Stitch
- ● Chain Stitch

MANDALA CUSHION

In Sanskrit the word 'mandala' means circle and this colourful design features rings of embroidery stitches radiating out from a buttonhole wheel centre. Start by raiding your crockery cupboard to find china with ever-increasing circumferences, from eggcups to cups, mugs, saucers, side and dinner plates, ready to mark out your design onto your fabric.

YOU WILL NEED

39cm (15½in) square of heavyweight woollen fabric

Two 39cm x 24cm (15½in x 9½in) pieces of heavyweight woollen fabric

Knitting wool (yarn) in a choice of colours

One or two large buttons

36cm (14in) square cushion pad

MAKING UP

1. Machine zigzag all around the edges of the square of woollen fabric to prevent fraying as you embroider.

2. Fold the fabric square into quarters and tack (baste) along the folds. Working through the marked centre point, fold along diagonal corners and tack (baste) as before to mark the eighths. This will help to keep everything square as you mark out and embroider the design.

3. To mark out the design, start by plotting out your circles onto a piece of paper (see Techniques: Marking out a circular shape). Starting from the centre, each disc needs to be a little larger than the one before it. When you are happy with your design, transfer it onto the fabric square, using a heat-erasable pen to draw around each circle, taking care to line up the stitching guidelines with the marked divisions on the fabric. Alternatively, use the template supplied (see Templates).

4. Using knitting wool (yarn), embroider your mandala design. See Embroidery Suggestions for possible stitch combinations, or make up your own using the Stitch Library and inspiration pages in this book: if you intersperse the radials with rows of running stitch it will help tie everything together visually (in fact, using just running stitch rounds throughout makes a simple starter mandala). Do experiment!

5. Once your embroidery is complete, unpick the tacking (basting) stitches and use a damp cloth to press the finished embroidery to remove the stitching guidelines, then make up as a cushion cover (see Techniques: Making a cushion cover).

EMBROIDERY SUGGESTIONS

Embroider your design using the stitch suggestions displayed here or in the alternative design provided. Refer to the Stitch Library for instructions for working the embroidery stitches.

- ● Buttonhole Wheel Stitch
- ● Eskimo Stitch
- ● Running Stitch
- ● Detached Chain Stitch
- ● Detached Fly Stitch
- ● Thorn Stitch

MANDALA CUSHION

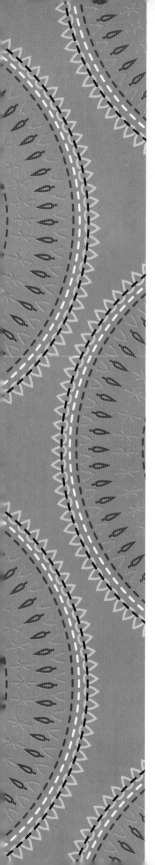

STYLISH SLIPPERS

A cosy pair of felt mule slippers will keep your toes toasty warm. If, like mine, your slippers need prettying up, a little hand-stitched embroidery is the perfect solution. The felt in this style of slipper tends to be very hard and thick, but this makes for speedier results as you will only be able to push the needle through the surface.

YOU WILL NEED

Felt slippers

Knitting or tapestry wool (yarn) in a choice of colours

MAKING UP

1. Make a copy of the stylish slippers bird template and enlarge or reduce to fit your slippers if necessary (see Techniques: Adapting the size of a paper template).

2. Cut out the main shapes of the bird motif and draw around them onto each of the slippers using a heat-erasable pen (see Techniques: Transferring a design). Remember to flip the design for the second slipper to give you a facing pair.

3. Using knitting or tapestry wool (yarn) in colours of your choosing, embroider the bird designs (see Embroidery Suggestions), working through the surface of the felt only.

4. Once you have embroidered the bird motifs on both slippers, fill in the background with a few cross stitches or star stitches and work whipped running stitch around the top edge of the slipper.

5. Once complete, use a damp cloth to press the finished embroidery to remove the pen markings.

At a glance

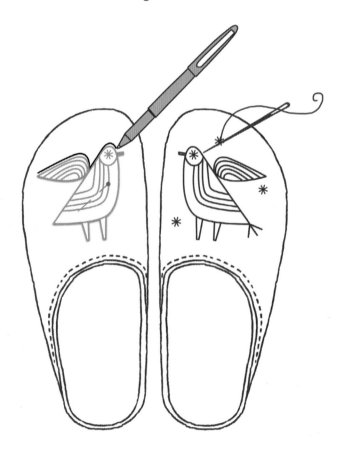

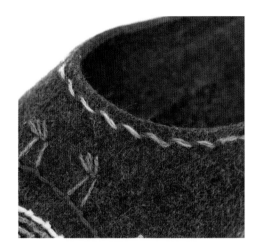

EMBROIDERY SUGGESTIONS

Embroider your design using the stitch suggestions displayed here. Refer to the Stitch Library for instructions for working the embroidery stitches.

- Cross Stitch
- Straight Stitch
- Coral Stitch
- Star Stitch

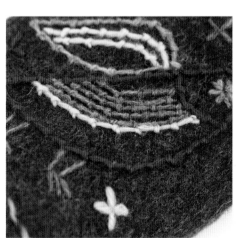

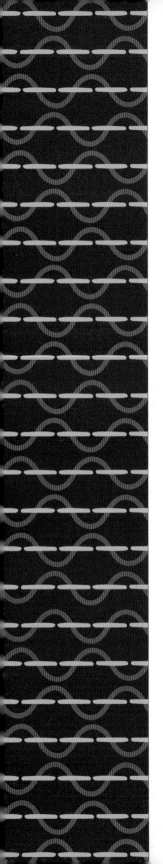

FOLK FLOWER MITTENS

We all need a sensible pair of fingerless gloves for winter crafting, but when simple mittens are embroidered with a sweet folk flower motif, they are elevated to an essential fashion accessory. The same design could be applied onto a knitted scarf and hat to make you a complete matching set.

YOU WILL NEED

Pair of knitted fingerless mittens

Knitting or tapestry wool (yarn) in a choice of colours

MAKING UP

1. Make a copy of the folk flower mittens template (see Templates) and enlarge or reduce to fit your mittens if necessary (see Techniques: Adapting the size of a paper template).

2. Cut out the main shapes of the flower motif and draw around them onto each mitten using a heat-erasable pen (see Techniques: Marking out a circular shape and Techniques: Transferring a design).

3. Using knitting or tapestry wool (yarn) in colours of your choosing, embroider the flower design on each mitten (see Embroidery Suggestions).

4. Once complete, use a damp cloth to press the finished embroidery to remove any pen markings.

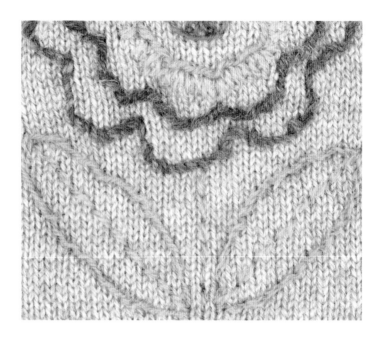

EMBROIDERY SUGGESTIONS

Embroider your design using the stitch suggestions displayed here. Refer to the Stitch Library for instructions for working the embroidery stitches.

- Detached Chain Stitch
- Whipped Running Stitch
- Lazy Daisy Stitch

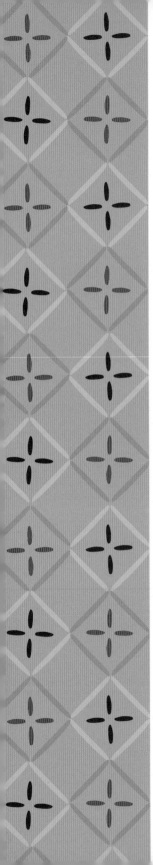

CHAIR BACK CUSHION

Here is a very simple design for a chair back cushion that you can make in just an evening or two. I have embroidered the colourful flat fish design with double knitting wool (yarn) but if you need your fish embroidery to be bigger, you can enlarge the template and use a thicker wool to embroider it with.

YOU WILL NEED

Two pieces of heavyweight linen or denim fabric sized to fit your chair back

Two strips of heavyweight linen or denim fabric for the ties (alternatively you can use cotton ribbon)

Iron-on interfacing

Knitting or tapestry wool (yarn) in a choice of colours

1.5cm (⅝in) thick blue upholstery foam sized to fit your chair back

MAKING UP

1. To determine the size of the fabric pieces you require, first measure the width and height of the area of the chair back where the finished cushion will sit and add 3cm (1¼in) to each measurement to allow for seam allowances. Use these measurements to cut out two pieces of heavyweight linen or denim fabric.

2. Make a copy of the chair back cover template (see Templates) and enlarge or reduce to fit one of your fabric panels (see Techniques: Adapting the size of a paper template), then cut it out.

3. Setting one of the fabric panels aside, prepare the other fabric panel for embroidery. Machine zigzag all around the edges to prevent fraying as you embroider and attach a piece of iron-on interfacing to the back (cut a little larger than the design motif) for stability.

4. Use a ruler and an air-erasable pen to draw a horizontal line in the centre of the prepared fabric panel. Take the cut out fish shape and use a heat-erasable pen to transfer it onto the fabric panel, lining up the centre of the fish with the centre guideline and filling in the internal details (see Techniques: Transferring a design).

5. Using knitting or tapestry wool (yarn), embroider the fish design (see Embroidery Suggestions).

6. Once you have completed the embroidery for the fish, work a double laced running stitch border at either side of the fish and fill in the background with a few lazy daisy stitches.

7. Once complete, use a damp cloth to press the finished embroidery to remove the pen markings.

8. To make the ties, I cut two strips of fabric approximately 4cm x 50cm (1½in x 20in), although you may need to adapt this measurement for your chair. Press a folded hem on the long edges of the two strips of fabric and at each short end. Fold the pieces in half lengthwise and machine stitch along the pressed hems.

9. Lay the embroidered piece of fabric right side facing up on your work surface and pin the folded ties to the top edge so that they point downwards. Now lay the set aside fabric panel on top, wrong side facing down. Pin and tack (baste) the front and back pieces together, and machine stitch with a 1.5cm (⅝in) seam allowance leaving a large turning gap at the bottom edge.

10. Trim the corners for a neat finish, then turn the cushion right sides out, carefully pushing out the corners to a point.

11. Cut a piece of foam just a little smaller than the cushion and slip it into the opening at the base of the cushion. Turn in the seam allowances at the opening and neatly hand stitch to close.

12. Attach the cushion to the chair by tying the fabric ties in neat bows.

At a glance

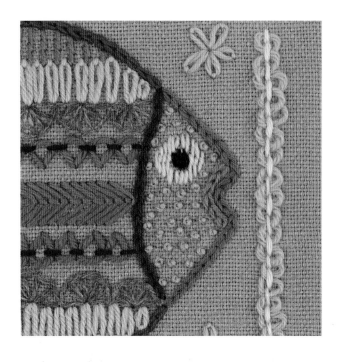

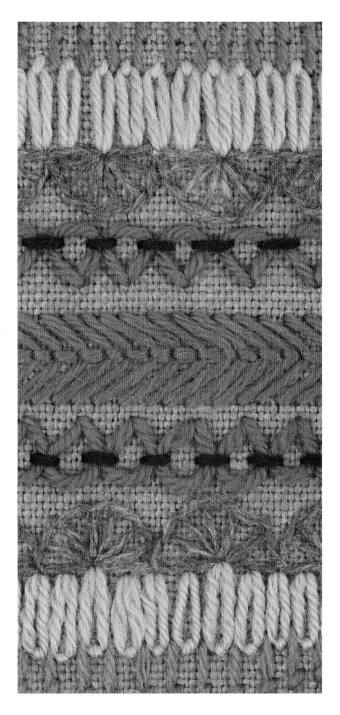

CHAIR BACK CUSHION

EMBROIDERY SUGGESTIONS

Embroider your design using the stitch suggestions displayed here. Refer to the Stitch Library for instructions for working the embroidery stitches.

- Lazy Daisy Stitch
- Chain Stitch
- Detached Chain Stitch
- Eskimo Stitch
- Fly Stitch
- Running Stitch

- French Knot
- Romanian Stitch
- Detached Fly Stitch
- Double Laced Running Stitch
- Buttonhole Wheel Stitch

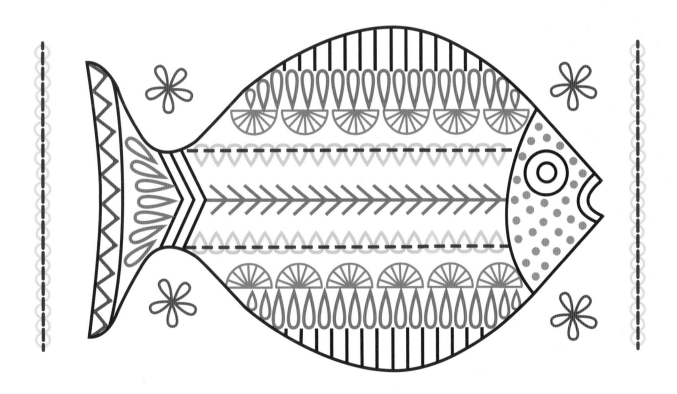

EMBELLISHED JEANS

Embroidery is a great way to extend the life of a much-loved pair of jeans. It's really up to you which stitches you use – think of it as working a sampler you can wear! I have embroidered a deep band on the hem of each leg and at the top edge of the back pocket, but where you embroider is your choice entirely.

YOU WILL NEED

Pair of jeans

Oddments of knitting or tapestry wool (yarn) in a choice of colours

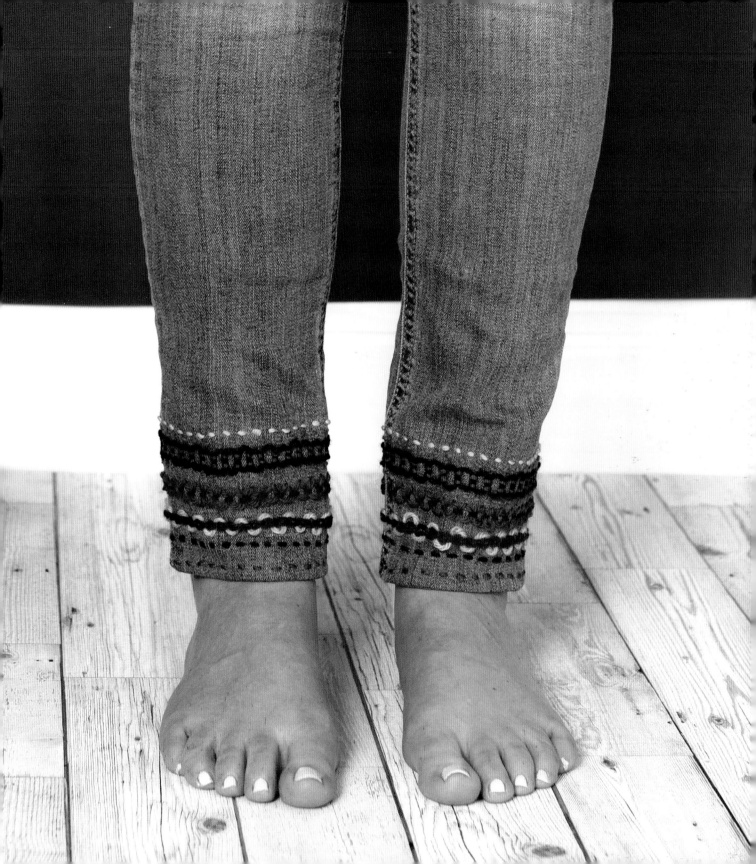

MAKING UP

1. Lay your jeans on a flat surface and use a ruler and a heat-erasable pen to mark out horizontal lines about 1cm (³⁄₈in) apart for each row of stitches you intend to embroider in the areas you have chosen to embellish. (If you prefer, you can draw these lines freehand, choosing any stitch combinations you wish to; remember that if you make a mistake the pen line will iron away, so you can begin again until you achieve the result you are after.)

2. Using knitting or tapestry wool (yarn), embroider your designs (see Embroidery Suggestions).

3. Once complete, use a damp cloth to press the finished embroidery to remove the stitching guidelines.

EMBROIDERY SUGGESTIONS

Embroider your design using the stitch suggestions displayed
here. Refer to the Stitch Library for instructions for working
the embroidery stitches.

- Herringbone Stitch
- Whipped Running Stitch
- Straight Stitch
- Eskimo Stitch
- Running Stitch
- Laced Chain Stitch
- Double Laced Running Stitch

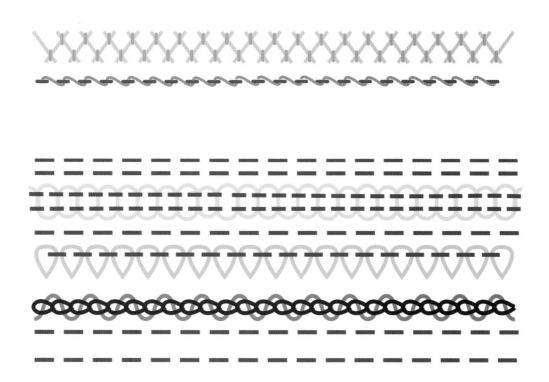

BUTTERFLY CUSHION

The bright, bold butterfly motif on this richly textured cushion takes only a little time to embroider. You can create your own variations simply by changing the thread colours and background fabric, or experiment with different stitches to make your own unique designs to bring a flight of butterflies to your soft furnishings.

– – – – – – – – –

YOU WILL NEED

43cm (17in) square of heavyweight woollen or linen fabric

Two 43cm x 27cm (17in x 10⅝in) pieces of heavyweight woollen or linen fabric

Knitting or tapestry wool (yarn) in a choice of colours

One or two large buttons

40cm (15¾in) square cushion pad

MAKING UP

1. Machine zigzag all around the edges of the square of woollen fabric to prevent fraying as you embroider.

2. Take your prepared fabric square and use a ruler and an air-erasable pen to draw a vertical line to mark the centre point.

3. Make a copy of the butterfly cushion template (see Templates) and join at the dashed red lines before cutting it out.

4. Line up the template against the marked centre line on the fabric and use a heat-erasable pen to draw around the cut out shape. Then flip the template to complete the butterly outline. Fill in the internal details and draw on the antennae (see Techniques: Transferring a design).

5. Using knitting or tapestry wool (yarn), embroider the butterfly design (see Embroidery Suggestions).

6. Once complete, use a damp cloth to press the finished embroidery to remove the pen markings, then make up as a cushion cover (see Techniques: Making a cushion cover).

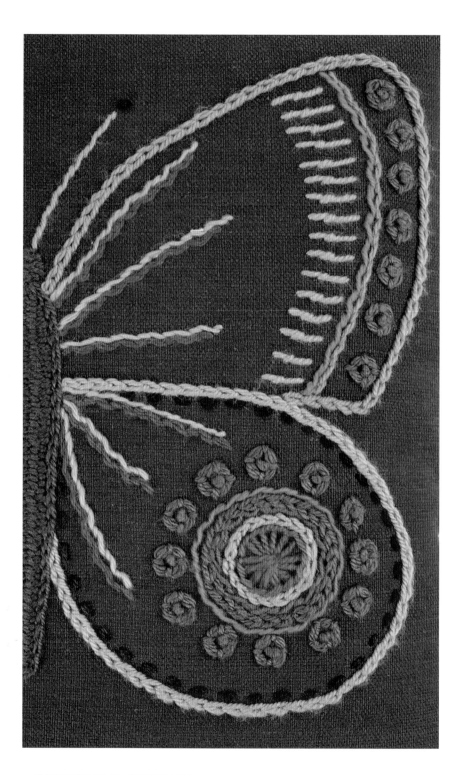

BUTTERFLY CUSHION

EMBROIDERY SUGGESTIONS

Embroider your design using the stitch suggestions displayed here. Refer to the Stitch Library for instructions for working the embroidery stitches.

- ● Romanian Stitch
- ● Chain Stitch
- ● Weave Stitch
- ● Whipped Running Stitch
- ● French Knot
- ● Buttonhole Wheel Stitch
- ● Running Stitch

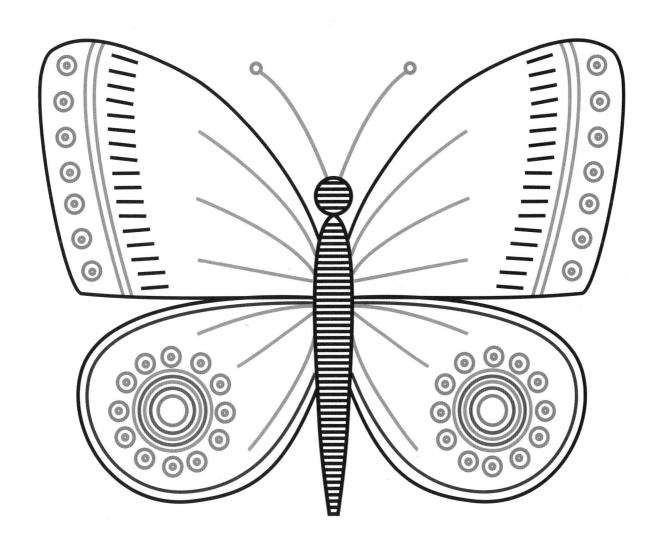

BIRD PICTURE

Here I have used the bird template from the stylish slippers project and adapted it to make a simple sampler picture using just a few decorative stitches. I chose an even weave upholstery fabric to make it easier to get even stitches by following the warp and weft of the fabric. Why not have a go at designing your own sampler picture?

YOU WILL NEED

Heavyweight linen fabric, cut to fit your picture frame aperture plus 5cm (2in) all around to allow for finishing

Knitting or tapestry wool (yarn) in a choice of colours

Picture frame

Mount card cut to fit your picture frame aperture

Masking tape

MAKING UP

1. Make a copy of the bird picture template (see Templates) and enlarge it to fit your frame (see Techniques: Adapting the size of a paper template). My frame measures approximately 16cm x 22cm (6¼in x 8⅝in).

2. Cut out the basic shapes and draw around them onto the fabric using a heat-erasable pen, roughly marking out where all the internal detailing will go (see Techniques: Transferring a design).

3. Using knitting or tapestry wool (yarn), embroider the bird design (see Embroidery Suggestions).

4. Once complete, use a damp cloth to press the finished embroidery to remove the pen markings.

5. Stretch the finished embroidery over the mount card (see Techniques: Mounting an embroidery design), and fit the mounted embroidery into your frame.

EMBROIDERY SUGGESTIONS

Embroider your design using the stitch suggestions displayed here. Refer to the Stitch Library for instructions for working the embroidery stitches.

- ● Chain Stitch
- ● French Knot
- ● Straight Stitch
- ● Star Stitch
- ● Couching Stitch
- ● Fly Stitch
- ● Laced Chain Stitch
- ● Stem Stitch
- ● Buttonhole Flower Stitch
- ● Back Stitch ⎫ worked together
- ● Cross Stitch ⎭ to create grid

KNITWEAR MOTIF

Embroidery is an easy way to add colour to a monochrome knitted garment. I have mirrored the twisting cables of this hand-knitted cardigan with a meandering flower stalk to connect the various elements of my floral motif. But this is just a happy starting point and you can make your own connections between texture and design.

— — — — — — — — —

YOU WILL NEED

Knitted garment of your choice

Knitting or tapestry wool (yarn) in a choice of colours

MAKING UP

1. Make a copy of the knitwear motif template (see Templates) and enlarge or reduce to fit your knitted garment if necessary (see Techniques: Adapting the size of a paper template). (Alternatively, create your own motif using any of the designs included in this book.)

2. Cut out around the outline of the flower head and leaf shapes and pin them in place as desired on your knitted garment, then refer to Embroidery Suggestions to embroider around these shapes using knitting or tapestry wool (yarn) in colours to complement your

knitwear. (As the texture of my knitted garment is quite chunky, I have worked the embroidery with double knitting wool (yarn), but modify your wool (yarn) choice to suit your knitted garment – for example, 4-ply (fingering) may be better suited for a finer knit to give a more delicate effect.)

3. Unpin the flower head and leaf shapes and trim them back to the internal flower head and leaf shapes and re-pin in place over the part-embroidered motifs, and embroider around these shapes as before.

4. Remove the pinned shapes and continue the embroidery to fill in the details on the flower heads and leaves. Connect the embroidered flowers and leaves with a twisting (chain stitch) stalk and finish by working the small buttonhole flower background details.

5. Once complete, use a damp cloth to press the finished motif.

EMBROIDERY SUGGESTIONS

Embroider your design using the stitch suggestions displayed here. Refer to the Stitch Library for instructions for working the embroidery stitches.

- ● Chain Stitch
- ● French Knot
- ● Straight Stitch
- ● Buttonhole Flower Stitch

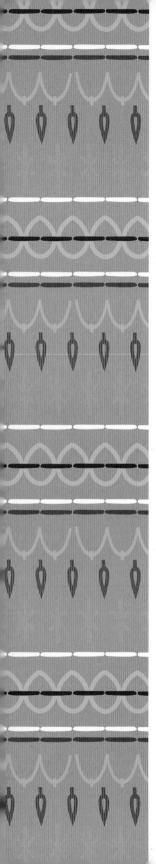

CROSSBODY PURSE

The shape and style of this little bag is reminiscent of Scandinavian waist purses – a colourful source of inspiration for traditional embroidery patterns. Its circular motifs look elaborate but are in fact very simple to stitch. Made from hard-wearing woollen fabric, it has a pretty cotton lining, an expandable drawstring opening and a practical carrying strap.

YOU WILL NEED

Two pieces of heavyweight woollen fabric approx 25cm (10in) square for outer bag

Two pieces of lightweight cotton fabric 25cm (10in) square for lining

Two pieces of lightweight cotton fabric approx 15cm (6in) square for drawstring flap

Knitting or tapestry wool (yarn) in a choice of colours

60cm (24in) length of narrow ribbon for drawstring closure

Bias tape for binding

Small piece of felt for strap attachment loops

Two D rings

Grosgrain ribbon for carrying strap, width as preferred and length cut to fit body shape

MAKING UP

1. Make a copy of the crossbody purse bag body template (see Templates) and cut out.

2. Use the bag body template to cut a front and back outer from the heavyweight woollen fabric pieces and two lining pieces from the larger lightweight cotton fabric pieces, placing the pattern on the fold of each of the pieces of fabric.

3. Take one of the outer (woollen fabric) pieces and prepare for embroidery, using the stitching guidelines on the pattern to help you mark out the circle motifs and lines of running stitch below (see Techniques: Marking out a circular shape and Techniques: Transferring a design). This will become the bag front.

4. Using knitting or tapestry wool (yarn), embroider the design that you have just marked out onto the bag front (see Embroidery Suggestions). If you choose to you can also mark and embroider lines of running stitch across the bag back.

5. Once complete, use a damp cloth to press the finished embroidery to remove the pen markings.

Note: You can enlarge or reduce the template to any size you choose to make a larger or smaller bag (see Techniques: Adapting the size of a paper template). This will affect the quantities of fabric you require, so you will need to make the necessary adjustments to make the purse to your preferred size, and the seamlines on the template will need to be adjusted to remain at approx 1.5cm (⅝in).

6. Place the bag front and bag back together, with right sides facing, and sew around the edge with a 1.5cm (⅝in) seam allowance leaving the top edge open. Trim the seam allowance and clip curves.

7. Repeat step 6 for the lining pieces.

8. Turn the outer bag right side out and insert the lining into the outer bag, wrong sides together.

9. Cut the cotton fabric pieces for the drawstring flap to size. These should measure the width of the bag plus 2cm (¾in) for hemming, and a little over half the bag's height. On each drawstring flap fabric piece, press and sew a 1cm (⅜in) hem along one short edge and each long edge. Fold over the hemmed short edge by 4cm (1½in) and sew in place to make the drawstring casing.

10. Position the prepared drawstring flap pieces at the top edge of the front and back of the bag, with right sides facing and raw edges aligned, and sew in place along the seamline. Bind all raw edges with bias tape (see Techniques: Binding an edge).

11. Thread the narrow ribbon through each side of the drawstring casing and tie the ends together with a small knot, then pull the ribbon around to lose the knot in one of the casing strips, leaving a ribbon loop at each side.

12. Cut a small strip of felt a little narrower than your D ring. Thread the felt strip through the D ring and stitch the ends of the felt together to make a strap attachment loop, and neatly hand stitch to the side seam just beneath the bound edge.

13. Thread one end of the grosgrain ribbon through one of the strap attachment loops and stitch in place. Repeat to attach the other end of the ribbon to the second strap attachment loop, adjusting the length as necessary before stitching in place.

At a glance

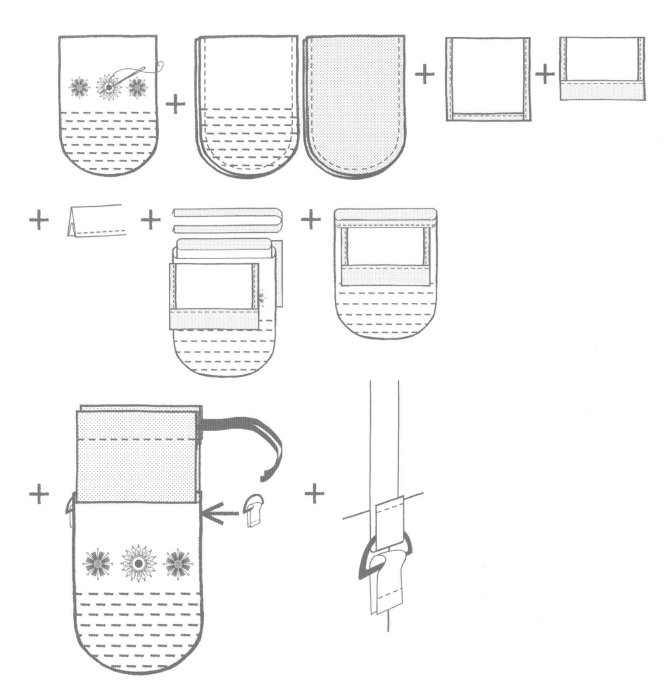

CROSSBODY PURSE

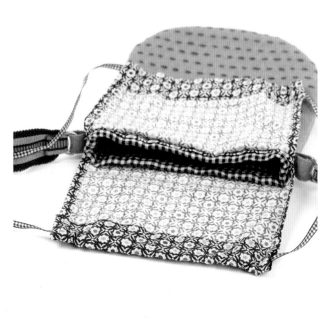

CROSSBODY PURSE

EMBROIDERY SUGGESTIONS

Embroider your design using the stitch suggestions displayed here. Refer to the Stitch Library for instructions for working the embroidery stitches.

- French Knot
- Back Stitch
- Satin Stitch
- Detached Chain Stitch
- Straight Stitch
- Romanian Stitch

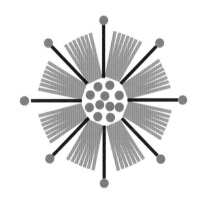

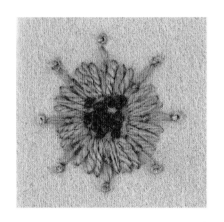

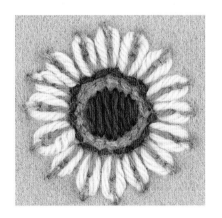

FLORAL SASH BELT

This beautiful fabric belt looks elaborate but is actually very easy to construct and it is sure to turn a simple dress or skirt into something special. The fabric requirements given are to make the belt as shown, but the pattern can be adapted to fit most waistlines, and the floral embroidery is worked with a fine yarn for lots of detail in the stitching.

– – – – – – – – –

YOU WILL NEED

Heavyweight woollen fabric approx 34cm x 14cm (13½in x 5½in) for the front belt panel

Lightweight cotton fabric approx 34cm x 14cm (13½in x 5½in) for the lining

Felt approx 34cm x 14cm (13½in x 5½in) for interlining

Knitting or tapestry wool (yarn) in a choice of colours

Bias binding to complement the front belt panel

Small pieces of felt for the belt loops

Two wide strips of lightweight cotton fabric for the sash (these should be long enough to go around your waist and be tied in a bow)

MAKING UP

1. Make a copy of the floral sash belt template (see Templates) and cut it out.

2. Use the belt template to cut out a front belt panel from the heavyweight woollen fabric, a lining panel from the lightweight cotton fabric and an interlining panel from the felt, placing the pattern on the fold of each of the pieces of fabric.

3. Mark centre guidelines on the front belt panel using a ruler and an air-erasable pen. Cut out the main shapes for the embroidery from the belt template and, using the marked centre lines as a guide, use a heat-erasable pen to draw around the main shapes onto the front belt panel, flipping the shapes to create a symmetrical design; then fill in the inner and background details (see Techniques: Transferring a design).

4. Using knitting or tapestry wool (yarn), embroider the marked out design (see Embroidery Suggestions).

5. Once complete, use a damp cloth to press the finished embroidery to remove the pen markings from the front panel.

6. Sandwich the felt interlining between the embroidered front panel and the lining, right sides facing out. Use the bias binding to bind the raw edges of the belt sandwich, making sure that the pieces are neatly aligned and taking care at the corners (see Techniques: Binding an edge).

At a glance

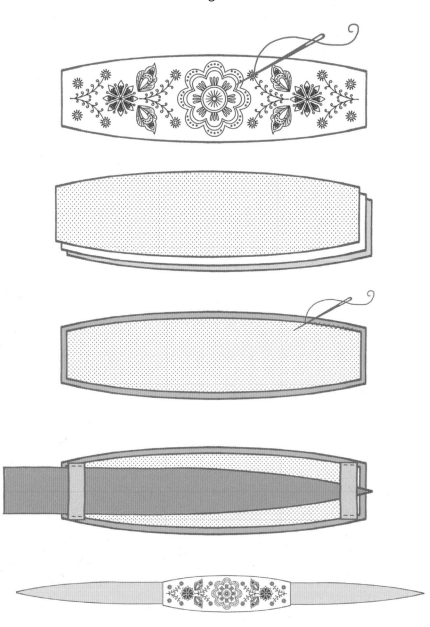

7. Use the belt loop template (see Templates) to cut the felt pieces to make the belt loops (depending on the quality of your felt, you may need to oversew two matching pieces of felt together to create each tab). Stitch the belt loops onto the back of the belt panel, one at each end.

8. To make the sash, take the lightweight cotton fabric strips and cut to a pointed shape at each end. Place right sides together and sew all around the edge leaving an opening on one side. Turn the sash through to the right side, then turn in the raw edges of the turning gap, hand stitch closed and press for a neat finish.

9. Thread the sash through the belt loops and tie in a bow around your waist.

EMBROIDERY SUGGESTIONS

Embroider your design using the stitch suggestions displayed here. Refer to the Stitch Library for instructions for working the embroidery stitches.

- Buttonhole Flower Stitch
- French Knot
- Detached Chain Stitch
- Straight Stitch
- Back Stitch
- Chain Stitch

BRIGHT BLANKET

If you want to explore how embroidery can be worked to follow the existing patterns in a woven blanket to create a bespoke throw, simply pick your blanket and let it dictate the design that is the perfect fit for it. The chevron weave in mine suggested a simple one-stitch zigzag repeated in a rainbow of vibrant colours.

YOU WILL NEED

Blanket

Knitting or tapestry wool (yarn) in a choice of colours

MAKING UP

1. First, choose your blanket. Keep a look out for throws that have a distinctive weave that suggest the pattern you could stitch, like the strong chevron weave on my chosen blanket. A tartan blanket is a good choice as the grid in the weave will naturally suggest many more design possibilities.

2. Essentially, now all you need to do is to choose a stitch to match the weave of your chosen blanket and get to work embroidering it. However, if you are not confident about the effect that will be achieved, you can map out your intended design onto the blanket using tacking (basting) stitches or, alternatively, use a heat-erasable marking pen.

3. As most blankets are made up of a complex weave, there is space between the warp and weft to hide the back of your stitches as you work. However, not all stitches can be hidden. I prefer to use surface stitches like couching stitch, laced running stitch and whipped running stitch – which is the stitch I have used to embroider this blanket – so that the reverse is magically unstitched while all the embroidered decoration is resplendent on the front. Some examples of other linear stitch designs that you might like to try on your blanket are pictured opposite.

4. Embroider your design using your chosen stitch in colours of your choosing. (If the weave of your chosen blanket is particularly fine, you may want to use finer crewel wool (yarn).) Refer to the Stitch Library for instructions for working the embroidery stitches suggested in step 3.

5. Once your embroidery is complete, unpick the tacking (basting) stitches, or use a damp cloth and a hot iron to iron out any pen mark guidelines.

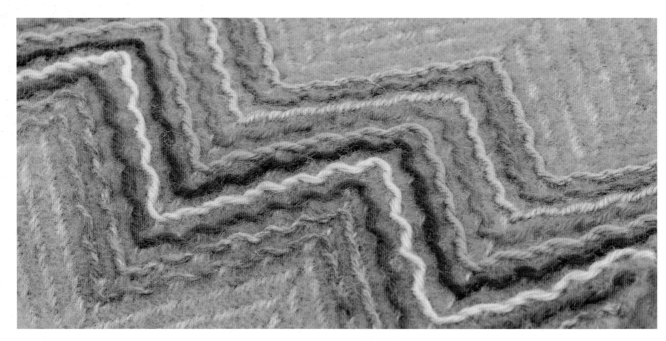

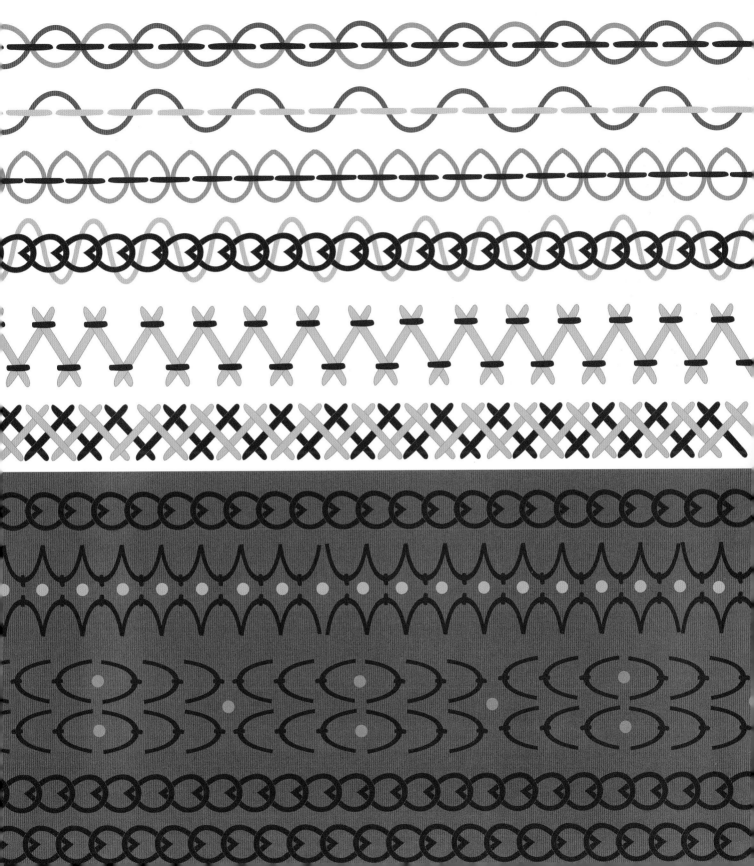

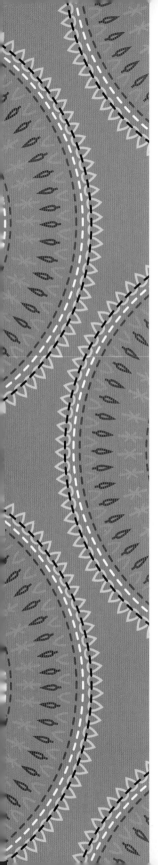

PEGBOARD SAMPLER

This unique piece of textile art is embroidered onto a pegboard that provides a background grid over which to work simple cross stitch. Stitching the cross stitch in blocks of colour to build up a pictorial design is really quite addictive, so much so that, as well as the house sampler photographed here, I have provided a second design for you to try.

– – – – – – – – – – –

YOU WILL NEED

Pegboard (from any good building materials supplier)

Paint (optional)

Air-erasable pen (optional)

Knitting or tapestry wool (yarn) in a choice of colours

Masking tape

MAKING UP

1. If you choose to, you can paint the pegboard first in a colour to set off the shades of your wools (yarns), but take care to apply light coats so as not to clog the holes of the pegboard with paint.

2. Before starting the embroidery, you might want to mark out your design with an air-erasable pen, so you can work quickly and be sure of where to place the blocks of different coloured cross stitch.

3. Use knitting or tapestry wool (yarn) to embroider the house design (see House Design). I used three strands of double knitting wool but a chunky wool (yarn) would work well too. When starting a new thread length, it's a good idea to tape the knots to the back of the pegboard to prevent them from pulling through the holes.

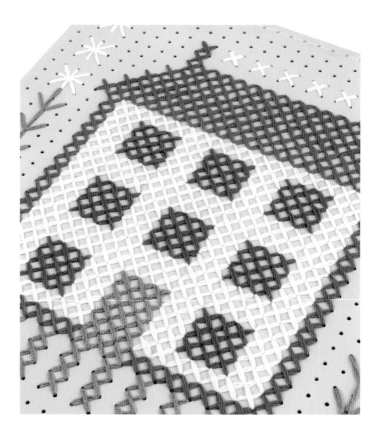

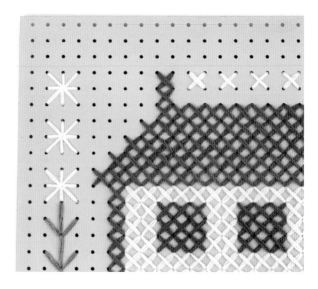

HOUSE DESIGN

This is a realistic representation of the finished house design as I have stitched it, showing the wool (yarn) colours that I stitched it in. You can, of course, choose your own colours. The white dots represent the holes in the pegboard through which you are working your stitches. The majority of the design uses cross stitch worked in rows, and the plants that border the house at each side are created with star stitch for the flowers and fly stitch for the stalks. Refer to the Stitch Library for instructions for working the embroidery stitches.

BIRD DESIGN

You can use the same technique to stitch this simple bird design, which is a version of the motif used for the child's skirt. The majority of the design is worked in cross stitch, with star stitch used for the bird's eye and tail feather detailing, and two horizontal rows of fly stitch create the wing detail on the bird's body. Refer to the Stitch Library for instructions for working the embroidery stitches.

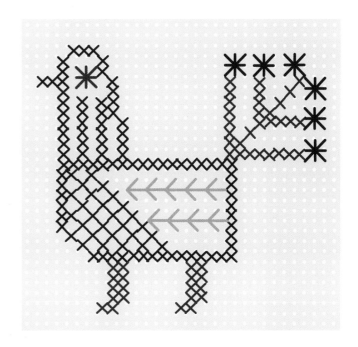

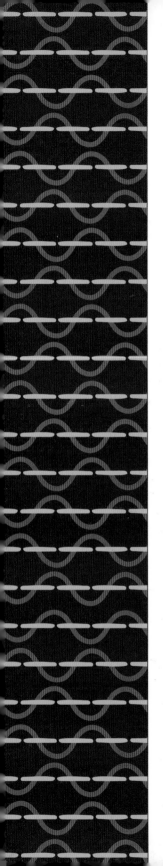

FLOWER CUSHION

Although I was only a child in the 1960s, this period still influences much of what I do, as is apparent in this design. I have used leftover yarn from my crochet basket, alongside some tapestry wool I had lying around, although six-strand embroidery cotton (floss) could be substituted here and there, particularly for the French knots.

YOU WILL NEED

43cm (17in) square of heavyweight linen fabric

Two 43cm x 27cm (17in x 10⅝in) pieces of heavyweight linen fabric

Knitting or tapestry wool (yarn) in a choice of colours

One or two large buttons

40cm (15¾in) square cushion pad

MAKING UP

1. Machine zigzag all around the edges of the square of linen fabric to prevent fraying as you embroider.

2. Take your prepared fabric square and use a ruler and an air-erasable pen to draw a vertical line to mark the centre point.

3. Make a copy of the flower cushion template (see Templates) and join at the dashed red lines, then cut out the main shapes.

4. Using the marked centre line as a guide, use a heat-erasable pen to draw around the cut out shapes, then mark out roughly where all the internal shapes and detailing will go (see Techniques: Transferring a design).

5. Using knitting or tapestry wool (yarn), embroider the flower design (see Embroidery Suggestions).

6. Once complete, use a damp cloth to press the finished embroidery to remove the pen markings, then make up as a cushion cover (see Techniques: Making a cushion cover).

EMBROIDERY SUGGESTIONS

Embroider your design using the stitch suggestions displayed here. Refer to the Stitch Library for instructions for working the embroidery stitches.

- Lazy Daisy Stitch
- Chain Stitch
- Back Stitch
- Eskimo Stitch
- Fly Stitch
- Weave Stitch
- French Knot

- Coral Stitch
- Herringbone Stitch
- Couching Stitch
- Romanian Stitch
- Whipped Running Stitch
- Stem Stitch
- Buttonhole Stitch

FLOWER CUSHION

TASSEL DECORATIONS

Using scraps of felt and wool, these tassels are so simple and satisfying to make – a great way to use up leftovers. The largest tassel can be used as a curtain tieback, and the smallest as a rustic Christmas decoration or blind pull. Why not make them in a range of different colours and string together to form bunting?

YOU WILL NEED

Felt in a choice of colours

Craft foam

Oddments of knitting or tapestry wool (yarn)

Chunky yarn for making the tassels

Cardboard

Ribbon approximately 20cm (8in) long

MAKING UP

Note: Instructions are given to work the large tassel and you can scale down the fabric sizes given to create smaller-sized tassels.

1. For the largest tassel, cut two 23.5cm x 8.5cm (9¼in x 3⅜in) pieces of felt and one 23cm x 8cm (9in x 3⅛in) piece of craft foam.

2. Use a heat-erasable pen to mark out a diamond grid at your preferred scale onto one piece of the felt (I used a 2cm (¾in) grid). Embroider along the lines with a long running stitch with equal spaces in between.

3. Embroider using tapestry wool (yarn) and your own choice of stitches or refer to Embroidery Suggestions for inspiration.

4. Layer the foam between the two felt pieces and use a small overstitch to secure the layers together. Join the two short sides to make a cuff as shown, using overstitch to fasten securely.

5. Cut a piece of card about twice the length you want your tassel to be. Wrap chunky yarn around the piece of card until it reaches the desired thickness. Remove the yarn from the card and use another piece of yarn to tie a knot around the centre. Cut through the looped ends and pull into a tassel shape.

6. Thread the top of the tassel through the felt cuff. Tie a ribbon loop or bow to the top of the tassel if desired.

At a glance

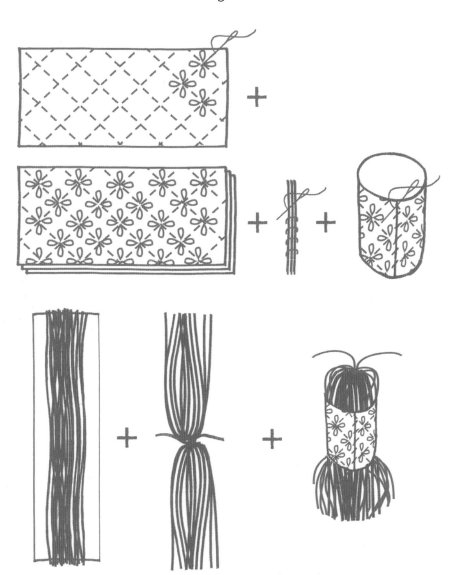

EMBROIDERY SUGGESTIONS

Embroider your design using the stitch suggestions displayed here. (Note: the smallest tassel was simply stitched with a row of star stitch.) Refer to the Stitch Library for instructions for working the embroidery stitches.

● Running Stitch   ● French Knot

● Lazy Daisy Stitch   ● Star Stitch

● Detached Chain Stitch   ● Straight Stitch

● Romanian Stitch

DRAWSTRING RUCKSACK

I used a boiled wool fabric to make this sweet rucksack, so there was no need to line it. The stitched decoration adds interest to this simple design and could incorporate any of the embroidery designs from this book. Once you have marked out the grid, you can quickly build up your pattern in stitches.

YOU WILL NEED

Two 35cm x 45cm (13¾in x 17¾in) pieces of heavyweight woollen fabric

Two 32cm x 12cm (12½in x 4¾in) pieces of lightweight cotton fabric

Two 6cm x 164cm (2½in x 64½in) strips of lightweight cotton fabric

Two 9cm (3½in) squares of lightweight cotton fabric

Knitting or tapestry wool (yarn) in a choice of colours

Scraps of ribbon

MAKING UP

1. Use a heat-erasable pen to mark out a 4cm (1½in) diamond grid pattern onto the bottom half of one piece of the heavyweight woollen fabric.

2. Using tapestry wool (yarn), embroider the design (see Embroidery Suggestions); the running stitches can be quite large, approx 1cm (⅜in) with equal spaces in between.

3. To make the tabs, press a 1.5cm (⅝in) folded hem on the long edges of the small lightweight cotton fabric squares. Fold in half lengthwise and machine stitch along the pressed hems to secure.

4. Place the woollen fabric pieces together, right sides facing. Fold each tab in half widthwise and pin in between the fabric layers at the bottom corners. Machine stitch around the bag using a 1.5cm (⅝in) seam allowance, leaving the top open.

5. To make the gathering band, press a 1.5cm (⅝in) hem around the long and short edges of the two 32cm x 12cm (12½in x 4¾in) pieces of lightweight cotton fabric. Fold in half lengthwise; pin and tack (baste), then machine stitch to the top edges of the bag.

6. To make the straps, press a 1.5cm (⅝in) folded hem on the long edges of the remaining cotton fabric strips. Fold in half lengthwise and machine stitch along the pressed hem edges.

7. Thread one strap through the band on one side of the bag, then back through the other band, so that its ends are at the same side. Thread one end through the bottom corner tab and sew the ends together. Cover the join with ribbon if desired. Repeat for the other strap on the opposite side of the bag.

EMBROIDERY SUGGESTIONS

Embroider your design using the stitch suggestions displayed here. Refer to the Stitch Library for instructions for working the embroidery stitches.

● Running Stitch   ● Cross Stitch

● French Knot   ● Star Stitch

At a glance

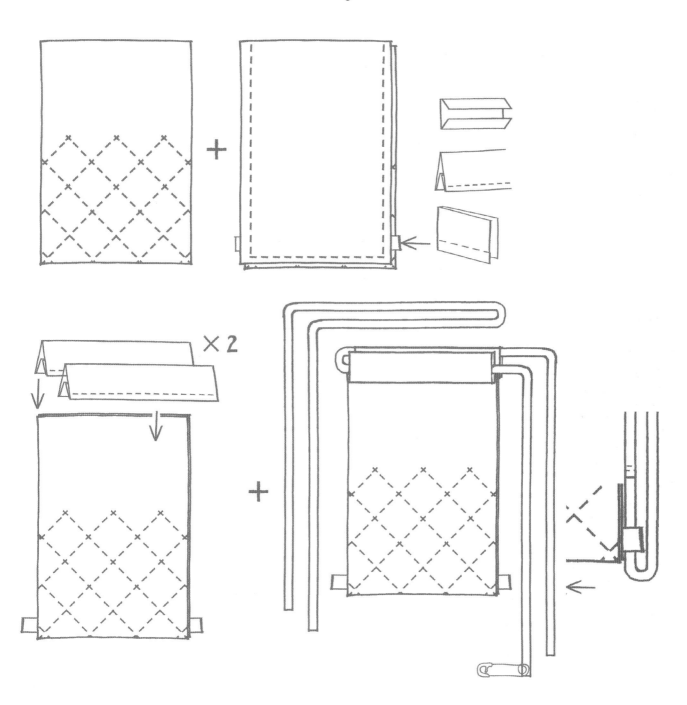

CHILD'S SKIRT

This sweet little skirt is like many that my mother made for me when I was very young. I remember one in particular made from a piece of beautiful Harris tweed with multi-coloured slubs. While the facing bird design looks great worked along the hem of a child's skirt, it would look just at home along a dress or coat hem, too!

- - - - - - - -

YOU WILL NEED

New Look Child's Easy Skirts Pattern No. 6486 or similar skirt pattern
Soft lightweight woollen fabric for making skirt according to chosen pattern
Knitting or tapestry wool (yarn) in a choice of colours

MAKING UP

1. Cut out and make up the skirt according to the pattern.

2. Use an air-erasable pen to draw a temporary straight line to help with the positioning of the embroidery motif. (I used the top fold of my skirt's hemline as my positioning guide.)

3. Make a copy of the child's skirt bird template (see Templates), then cut it out. Use this shape to draw pairs of facing birds along the hem of the skirt using a heat-erasable pen, then fill in the internal details and mark on the tail feather lines on each bird.

4. Using knitting or tapestry wool (yarn), embroider the facing birds design (see Embroidery Suggestions).

5. Once complete, use a damp cloth to press the finished embroidery to remove the pen markings.

At a glance

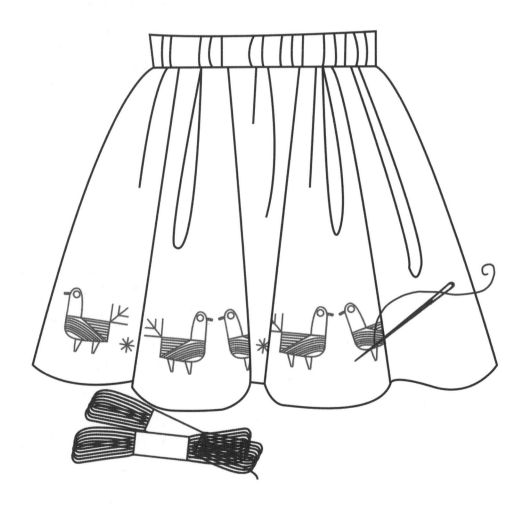

EMBROIDERY SUGGESTIONS

Embroider your design using the stitch suggestions displayed here. Refer to the Stitch Library for instructions for working the embroidery stitches.

● Back Stitch
● Straight Stitch
● Star Stitch

● Fly Stitch
● Romanian Stitch

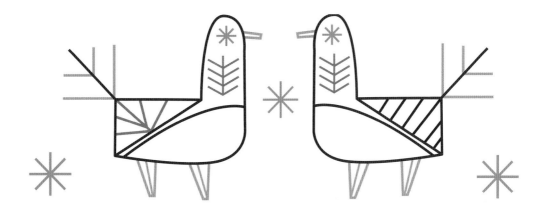

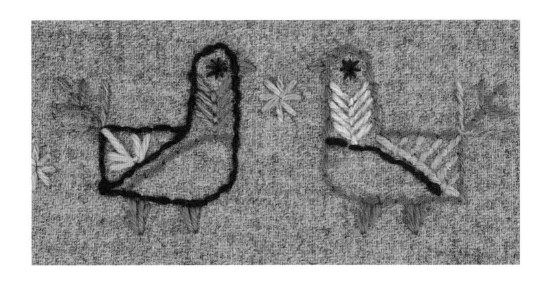

FELT DECORATIONS

To illustrate how versatile the embroidery motifs featured in this book are, I have reused two motifs to make a pair of hanging decorations from thick felt, although you could use several layers of standard felt sandwiched together if you prefer. I used simple stitches but you could add buttons, beads and sequins too!

YOU WILL NEED

Felt approximately 5mm (¼in) thick

Oddments of knitting or tapestry wool (yarn)

String for hanging loop

MAKING UP

1. Make a copy of the felt decorations templates (see Templates) and use to cut out one of each bird shape from thick felt.

2. Use a heat-erasable pen to mark out embroidery guidelines onto one side of the felt following the lines on the Embroidery Suggestions.

3. Using knitting or tapestry wool (yarn) in colours of your choosing, embroider the bird designs (see Embroidery Suggestions), working through the surface of the felt only. Keep your needle as horizontal as possible to make sure that none of your stitches show through on the back of the felt.

4. Once complete, use a damp cloth to press the finished embroidery to remove the pen markings.

5. Attach a length of string at the top centre point of each decoration for hanging.

Note: If using standard felt, cut out three of each shape and trim one set by 3mm (⅛in) all around to become the filling in your felt decoration sandwich. Embroider the front (and back if you choose to) of each shape, then sandwich the trimmed felt shape in between and oversew all around the edges using a cotton sewing thread to match the colour of your felt.

At a glance

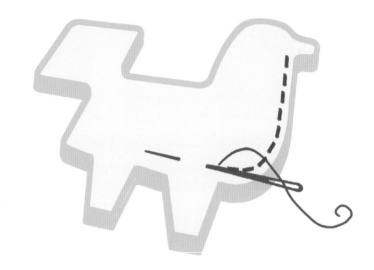

EMBROIDERY SUGGESTIONS

Embroider your design using the stitch suggestions displayed
here. Refer to the Stitch Library for instructions for working
the embroidery stitches.

- ● Whipped Running Stitch
- ● Fly Stitch
- ● Star Stitch
- ● Straight Stitch

FLOWER PICTURE

I love working on dark canvas with bright colours as the end result always looks so rich. My inspirations include traditional folk costume and Elizabethan embroidery, and these influences can be seen in my flower picture design, with a touch of sentimental nostalgia for 1970s embroidery too!

YOU WILL NEED

Heavyweight linen fabric, cut to fit your picture frame aperture plus 5cm (2in) all around to allow for finishing

Knitting or tapestry wool (yarn) in a choice of colours

Picture frame (I've made mine to fit an A3 picture frame but you can make yours any size you like)

Mount card cut to fit your picture frame aperture

Masking tape

MAKING UP

1. Make a copy of the flower picture template (see Templates) and join at the dashed red lines.

2. Cut out the basic shapes and draw around them onto the fabric using a heat-erasable pen, making sure all circular elements are marked (see Techniques: Transferring a design and Techniques: Marking out a circular shape).

3. Using knitting or tapestry wool (yarn), embroider the flower design (see Embroidery Suggestions).

4. Once complete, use a damp cloth to press the finished embroidery to remove the pen markings.

5. Stretch the finished embroidery over the mount card (see Techniques: Mounting an embroidery design), and fit the mounted embroidery into your picture frame.

EMBROIDERY SUGGESTIONS

Embroider your design using the stitch suggestions displayed here. Refer to the Stitch Library for instructions for working the embroidery stitches.

- ● Chain Stitch
- ● Whipped Running Stitch
- ● Straight Stitch
- ● Eskimo Stitch
- ● French Knot
- ● Detached Chain Stitch
- ● Thorn Stitch
- ● Buttonhole Flower Stitch

- ● Romanian Stitch
- ● Star Stitch
- ● Detached Fly Stitch
- ● Running Stitch
- ● Feather Stitch
- ● Herringbone Stitch

FLOWER PICTURE

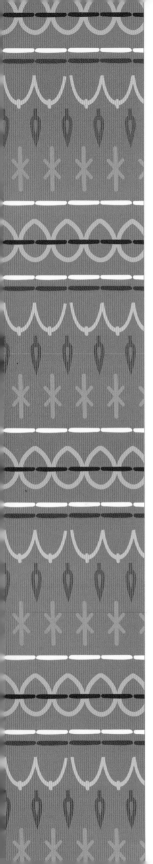

EMBROIDERY ON FABRIC

If you want to experiment further with hand-stitched embroidery, keep a look out for print fabrics, both retro and contemporary, where the patterns can be accentuated with embroidery stitches.

Vintage and retro fabrics, sourced from markets, second-hand and charity shops, often provide an ideal base for freestyle embroidery, and tea towels, in particular, have fantastic bold designs and colours that are perfect to use as a stitching background. There are also some great finds to be had in the oddments box in fabric shops and you only need a little to make a framed picture or a cushion cover.

Follow the contours of the fabric pattern and let the design dictate the stitches you work. Remember that stitches can be simple and still have great effect. Try different wool (yarn) thicknesses to see what results they will give you, or try combining some of the stitches you know to create new effects. Look for inspiration within the fabric. Once you start doing this you will see possibilities everywhere.

To prepare your fabric for embroidery, iron lightweight iron-on interfacing to the back for stability and zigzag around the edges to prevent fraying as you embroider. Then get creative!

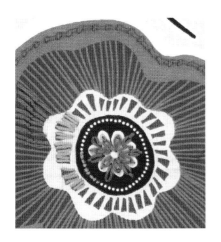

TECHNIQUES

ADAPTING THE SIZE OF A PAPER TEMPLATE

Most home printers today have a built-in scanner. Use this to scan the paper template you want to use, making sure you keep the page pressed as flat as possible. Then proceed in one of the following ways:

Method 1: Use the setting in your scanner controls to enlarge or magnify the image to the size you require then print it out.

Method 2: For more control, save the scanned page as an image on your computer ready to open up either with photo-editing software, or import into a word processing document, so that you can crop the image and/or enlarge it relative to an A4 (US letter) sheet of paper and print it out. (If you want to print larger than A4 (US letter) size, you'll need to use your printer's tiling capability and for this you should refer to your printer manual for instruction.)

If you don't have a home printer with a scanner, you'll need to take this book along to your local print or copy shop, along with the dimensions of the image you want to come away with.

TRANSFERRING A DESIGN

Cut out the main shapes of your paper template ready to transfer to your fabric.

When drawing around the shapes, work from a central point. If working from the centre of the fabric, fold it half and half again to make a light crease mark to guide you. Or use an air-erasable pen to mark centring guidelines. Then lay the paper pieces down and draw around them with a heat-erasable pen.

It is helpful to mark other elements lightly with a heat-erasable pen, which will help to guide you once you come to fill in the details by eye. Remember, you do not need to follow the pattern slavishly and you are encouraged to modify the designs as you choose to, even as you stitch.

MARKING OUT A CIRCULAR SHAPE

Fold the paper circle into quarters to find the middle.

Draw around the circle onto the fabric with an air-erasable pen, marking first the quarters then the eighths.

Once you have marked the fabric in this way, you can more confidently complete the embroidery.

MAKING A CUSHION COVER

Stitch a double hem on one long edge of the two cushion back fabric pieces, i.e., fold over by 1.5cm (⅝in) and then by the same amount again.

Machine one buttonhole in the centre of the hemmed edge of one of the pieces (or two buttonholes evenly spaced).

Sew button(s) to hemmed edge of remaining back piece to align with the buttonhole(s) and do up the button(s).

Lay embroidered front onto buttoned-up back, right sides facing. Pin and tack (baste) together, and machine stitch all around using a 1.5cm (⅝in) seam allowance.

Clip corners close to seam, but be careful not to go too close.

Undo button(s) and turn the cushion cover right side out. Press with a damp cloth to finish, then insert cushion pad.

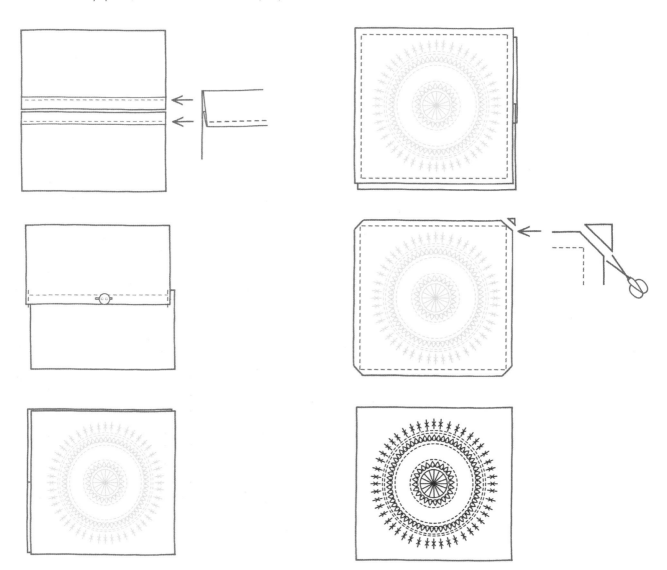

BINDING AN EDGE

Binding raw edges creates a neat decorative finish on projects such as the floral sash belt and the crossbody purse.

Unfold one of the pressed edges of the bias binding, align raw redges with right sides facing and machine stitch along the fold line.

Fold the binding over to the back of the project, concealing the raw edges, and neatly hand stitch in place.

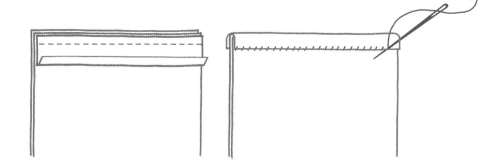

MOUNTING AN EMBROIDERY DESIGN

Make sure the mount card is the same internal size as your picture frame.

Centre the card on the back of the embroidery, turn over the top edge of the fabric and tape in place on the back of the card. Turn over the bottom edge, pull taut, and then tape in place.

Tape the sides of the fabric in the same way, then stitch the corners using overstitch.

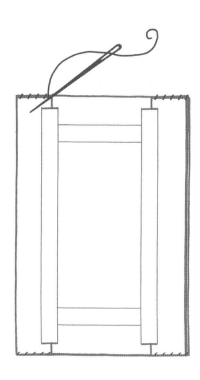

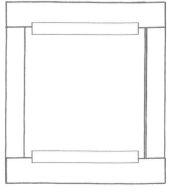

TEMPLATES

All templates are shown at actual size. Printable
versions of these templates can be downloaded from:
http://ideas.sewandso.co.uk/patterns.

STYLISH
SLIPPERS

KNITWEAR
MOTIF

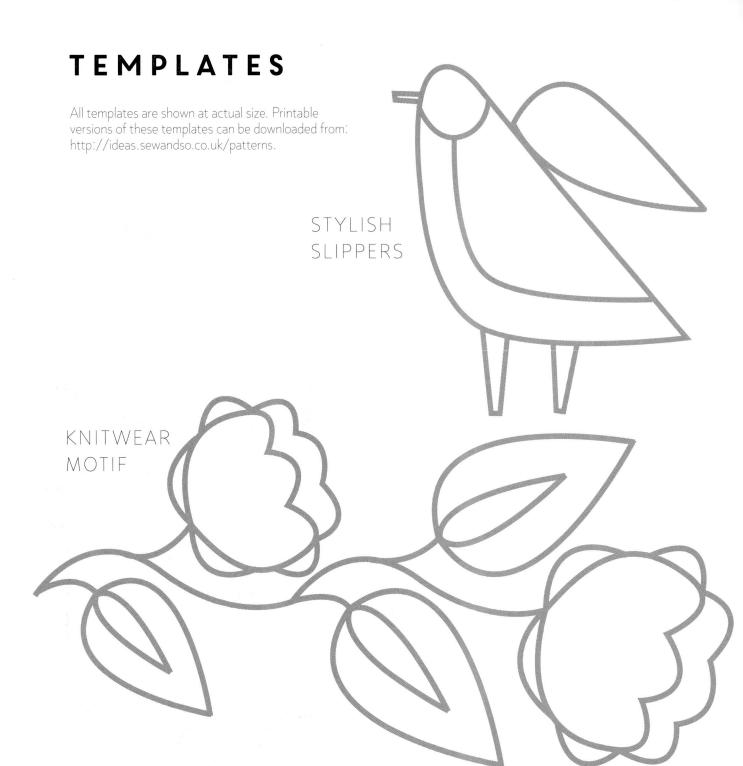

FELT DECORATIONS

FOLK FLOWER
MITTENS

FLOWER
PICTURE

Part A

join to Part B

join to Part C

join to Part A

FLOWER
PICTURE
Part B

join to Part D

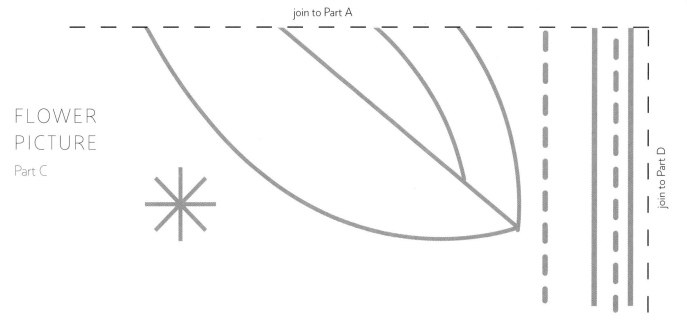

join to Part A

join to Part D

FLOWER PICTURE

Part C

FLORAL SASH BELT

seamline

place on fold

TEMPLATES

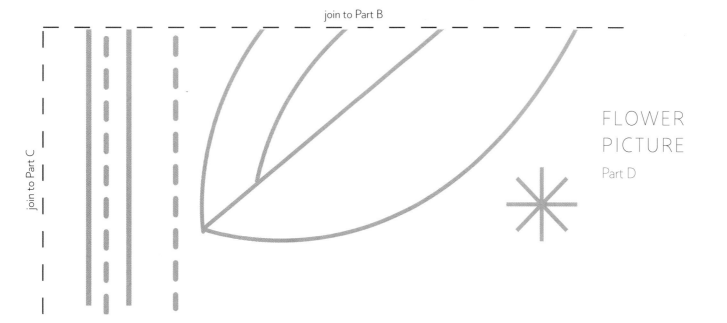

join to Part C

FLOWER PICTURE
Part D

FLORAL SASH BELT

Belt
Loop

CHILD'S SKIRT

MANDALA
CUSHION

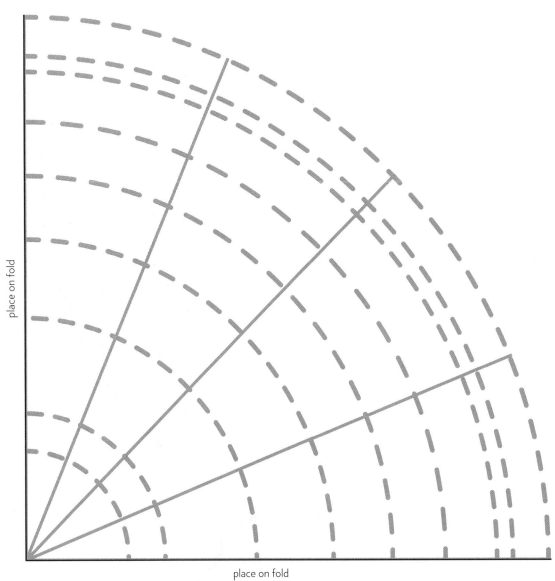

place on fold

place on fold

CHAIR BACK
CUSHION

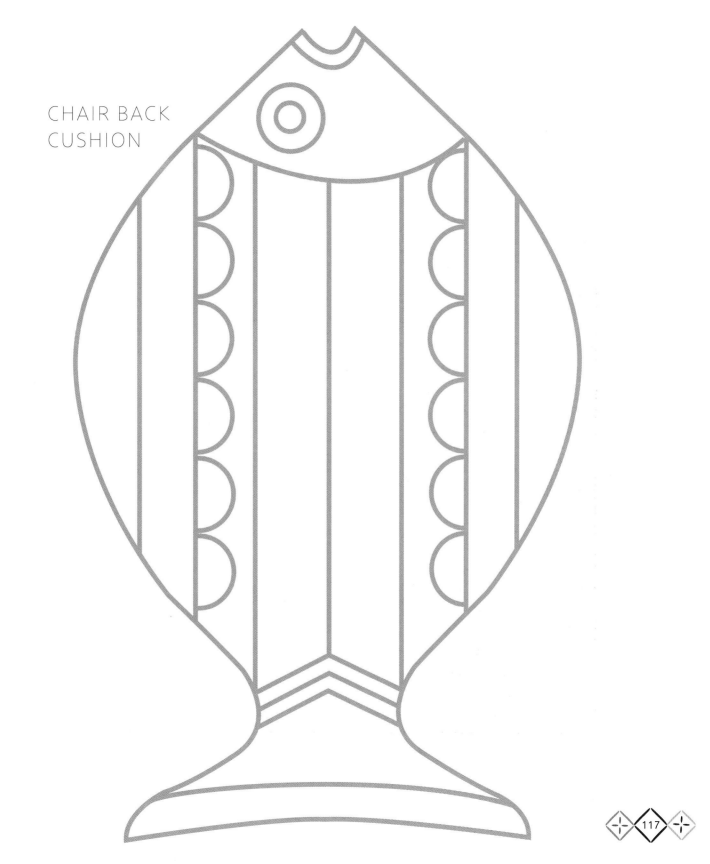

FLOWER CUSHION

Part A

join to Part B

join to Part C

join to Part A

join to Part D

FLOWER CUSHION

Part C

join to Part A

join to Part D

FLOWER CUSHION

Part D

join to Part B

join to Part C

BUTTERFLY CUSHION

Part A

place on fold

join to Part B

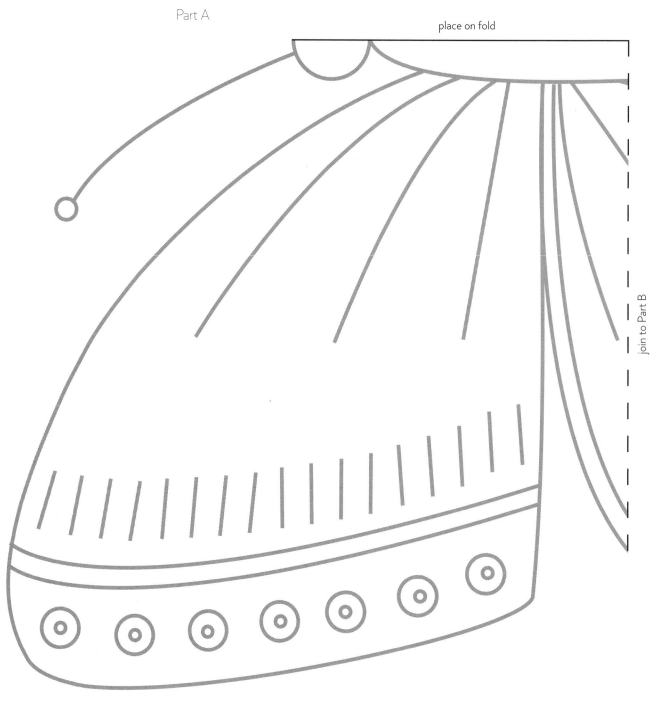

TEMPLATES

BUTTERFLY CUSHION

Part B

place on fold

join to Part A

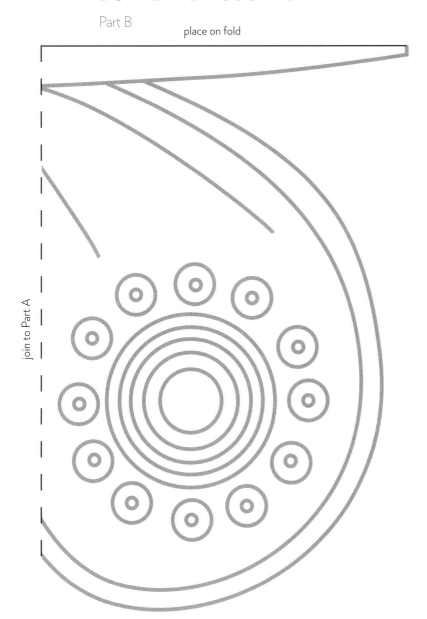

CROSSBODY PURSE
Bag Body

seamline

place on fold

BIRD
PICTURE

SUPPLIERS

SLIPPERS
www.seasaltcornwall.co.uk

LINEN FABRIC
www.merchantandmills.com

WOOLLEN FABRIC
www.merchantandmills.com
www.myfabrics.co.uk

COTTON FABRIC
www.sewandso.co.uk

CRAFT FOAM
www.hobbycraft.co.uk

FELT
www.buttoncompany.co.uk
www.cloudcraft.co.uk

ABOUT THE AUTHOR

Nancy Nicholson is a leading embroidery designer well known for her folk art inspired patterns and motifs. She has developed a unique and distinctive style for decorative embroidery that has a very modern aesthetic but is based on traditional techniques.

Nancy sells her designs and kits online and has a fast growing, loyal following of international fans. She has an impressive arts and crafts pedigree and is following in the footsteps of her mother, Joan Nicholson, an accomplished embroidery designer and author.

www.nancynicholson.co.uk

In memory of Biddy.

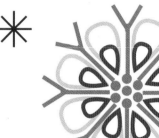

INDEX

A SEWANDSO BOOK
© F&W Media International, Ltd 2018

SewandSo is an imprint of F&W Media International, Ltd
Pynes Hill Court, Pynes Hill, Exeter, EX2 5AZ, UK

F&W Media International, Ltd is a subsidiary of F+W Media, Inc
10151 Carver Road, Suite #200, Blue Ash, OH 45242, USA

Text and Designs © Nancy Nicholson 2018
Layout and Photography © F&W Media International, Ltd 2018

First published in the UK and USA in 2018

A catalogue record for this book is available from the British Library.

ISBN-13: 978-1-4463-0713-7 paperback
SRN: R8068 paperback

ISBN-13: 978-1-4463-7712-3 PDF
SRN: R8107 PDF

ISBN-13: 978-1-4463-7711-6 EPUB
SRN: R8106 EPUB

Printed in China by RR Donnelley for:
F&W Media International, Ltd
Pynes Hill Court, Pynes Hill, Exeter, EX2 5AZ, UK

10 9 8 7 6 5 4 3 2 1

Content Director: Ame Verso
Acquisitions Editor: Sarah Callard
Managing Editor: Jeni Hennah
Project Editor: Cheryl Brown
Design Manager: Lorraine Inglis
Designer: Sam Staddon
Photographer: Jason Jenkins
Art Direction and Styling: Lorraine Inglis
Production Manager: Beverley Richardson

F&W Media publishes high quality books on a wide range of subjects.
For more great book ideas visit: www.sewandso.co.uk

Layout of the digital edition of this book may vary depending on reader hardware and display settings.